THE
Archive Photographs
SERIES
THE BOOK OF
THE AXE

This picture of the first lorry bought by the Axminster-based coal and builders merchants R.J. Luff, like many views of the lower Axe valley taken between 1900 and 1925, including several in this book, is the work of excellent local photographer Charles Humphries (1877-1959). Humphries (inset) was born in the Sherborne area and returned there to live with his grandmother after going to Australia and not liking the place. He moved to Axminster at the turn of the century and set up a photographer's business from his house in West Street. In later years he covered the area with an Indian motorcycle and sidecar. After the Second World War he was a pioneer of TV in Axminster. The lorry is photographed at the entrance to Axminster station in around 1920 outside the weighbridge office which belonged to rival coal and builders merchants Bradford & Son. Bradfords eventually had the last laugh though, taking over R.J. Luff in recent years.

THE
Archive Photographs
SERIES

THE BOOK OF
THE AXE

Compiled by
Les Berry and Gerald Gosling

CHALFORD

First published 1996
Copyright © Les Berry and Gerald Gosling, 1996

The Chalford Publishing Company
St Mary's Mill, Chalford,
Stroud, Gloucestershire, GL6 8NX

ISBN 0 7524 0775 9

Typesetting and origination by
The Chalford Publishing Company
Printed in Great Britain by
Redwood Books, Trowbridge

Silverleigh, Silver Street, Axminster, *c.* 1910. The house no longer has the creeper on its walls.

Contents

At a time when the entire red sandstone cliffs at Seaton Hole (centre background) are under considerable threat from the sea now that much of the beach has been washed away, it is interesting to note that the old West Walk (seen here in around 1902) was extended as far as the path ('Jacob's Ladder' in latter years) that went up to Old Beer Hill. Today the West Walk stops at the Chine. Mixed bathing was allowed at Seaton Hole because, as Seaton Urban District Council claimed, 'the town was anxious to keep abreast of the times and meet the wishes of her visitors'!

Introduction

When Adam and Eve were dispossessed
Of a garden hard by Heaven
They planted another down in the west
'Twas Devon, glorious Devon!

A century and a half ago, before the railways came to Devon, people lived in the same houses in the same villages and towns that their families had inhabited from time immemorial. There may have been dire rural poverty in those days but at least there was a feeling of permanence and of roots going down many feet into the rich red Devon soil.

A journey in 1840 still meant exactly what it means in French – how far one could travel in one day on one horse. From where I am writing, in the village of Uplyme, the furthest that anyone went in the course of the year in 1840 was to Honiton.

Exeter, which is twenty-nine miles away, was out of range. People were localized, as we can hear in their inherited, regional accents. Why else is the west Dorset dialect so different from the east Devon one? But the railways gave the population the chance to travel easily, comfortably, quickly and cheaply. People started to move.

One hundred years ago the cursed motor car with its insatiable desire for more and yet more roads arrived. Glorious Devon became less shipshape as its wonderful landscape began to be eaten up by the desires of the voracious automobile. Hedges went, fields were appropriated, cities were given one-way systems, and picturesque village high streets hosted traffic jams.

And with the motor car came two new species to Devon – the 'grockle', complete with caravan, and the 'retired' with his appetite for golf and bowls. East Devon today is inundated by ever-increasing hordes of tourists and an elderly retired population. Historic Devon was and is under siege.

And, by the way, by the year 2011, Government policy requires 90,000 new houses to be built in Devon. Where on earth will they all go? Will there be any of the Devon that we know and love left?

The past, which is receding so fast, needs to be recorded. Stop to sneeze and it is lost for ever. Eugene O'Neill said, 'The only living life is the past and the future; the present is an interlude.'

So it is right and proper that the authors should preserve for posterity this fascinating set of pictures with their perceptive and valid comments. If they had not done so, many of these views would have disappeared for ever. 'O call back yesterday, bid time return,' cries an anguished Richard II. But it is a futile plea. The past cannot be recalled; all that can be done is to recollect it as accurately as possible.

The authors have revived remembrance of things past with this beautiful book of pictures. For their time, trouble and patient scholarship we are all grateful. And as we look at their photographs with nostalgia and delight, we wonder if it is time to pull up the drawbridge against the invading masses. The message of the book is 'perhaps, maybe, but not yet'.

Jack Thomas
Uplyme, 1997

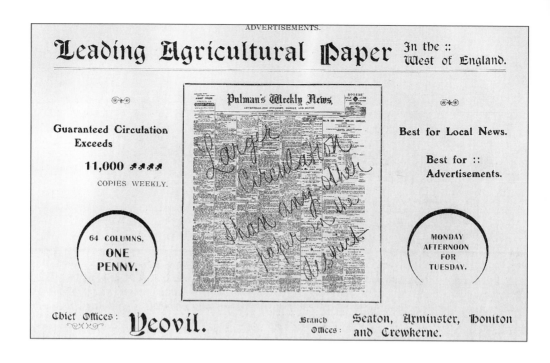
In 1844 George Pulman produced his *The Book of the Axe*, which, though not always accurate, has long since been accepted as the best account of the tiny river born in the hills above Beaminster which meanders through south-west Somerset before discharging into the English Channel east of Seaton.

The Book of the Axe ran into several editions, including a complete reprint in 1975, and on the rare occasions a first edition appears on the market it fetches upwards of a thousand pounds. The first two editions were slim volumes. In 1854 a third and much larger edition appeared. It had been so re-written and enlarged that Pulman said of it 'the title alone is almost the only original feature'. And of the fourth edition, first published in twelve separate parts between January 1873 and February 1875, he said 'it contains nearly four times as much matter as the third edition'.

We have set out a century and a half later to retrace George Pulman's footsteps in old photographs of the parishes of the lower Axe, from where it crosses the Somerset border down to its mouth. In a second and later volume we will cover the river from its source to the end of its Somerset stretch.

One

Chardstock and Hawkchurch

Chardstock, c.1906.

The George Inn, Chardstock, c. 1948. The George was once the Church House and is said to date back to the thirteenth century and even before. It has a crypt under the lounge and its own ghost, a monk, who appears from time to time.

St Andrew's church, Chardstock, c. 1905. St Andrew's was considerably renovated in 1863 with the usual Victorian lack of feeling. Outside, however, it manages to look quite impressive. The renovation was the brainchild of the Revd Charles Woodcock (vicar 1834-75) who was also responsible for rebuilding the vicarage, adding bits to the National School and building St Andrew's College in 1865. The college, which closed in 1885, offered schooling to children who had lost fathers in the Crimean War and had as many as 230 pupils at one stage.

Hawkchurch, *c.* 1905. The donkey-drawn mail cart made the journey from Axminster every day. George Pulman claims that the the Old Inn, 'occupied as an inn from times immemorial', and four other cottages and the parish poorhouse were destroyed in a deliberately started fire in 1806. The inn was 'probably erected for the accommodation of the tenants of the rector's manor at the time of the courts, and for use by other parishioners at wedding feasts and other public and festive occasions'.

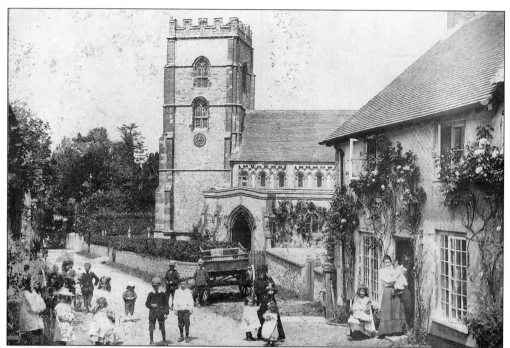

Hawkchurch, c. 1899. In the background is a wagon belonging to Mr Sampson, the local miller. In front of it are the Hayball twins, George and Len. St John the Baptist's church in the background has had three different dedications. In Norman times it was All Saints' church; then it was changed to St Peter's.

St John the Baptist's church before it was almost completely rebuilt between 1859-60 by the rector, the Revd E. Cay Adams, who had offered to stand the cost if the Vestry would allow him a free hand and £250. He only got the free hand. Sadly, a singers' gallery in the tower opening to the nave disappeared at the time, as did the door to the tower ringing chamber and the rood screen in the north aisle. Cay Adams did build a larger chancel and brought more light into the church after he raised the walls and roof to make room for a clerestory.

Unfortunately this postcard of Hawkchurch Branch No. 362 does not say what it was a branch of. Take your pick: Foresters, Friendly Society or Village Club? All that is known is that it dates from before the 2 July 1906 postmark on this card sent to Warwick by, presumably, some one staying at Bridport.

Hawkchurch, c. 1938. The name Hawkchurch probably comes from the Old English personal name 'heafoc', a hawk, and this would indicate the existence of a church here from Saxon times, a fact borne out by the Saxon font.

Wyld Court, Hawkchurch, *c.* 1890. Amos Mullins is the man with his hands on the gatepost. Wyld Court was built by a John Leigh who acquired the manor after the Dissolution. It went to the Moore family, and the initials TM with the date 1593 on a lead pipe are probably those of Thomas Moore. Henry VI granted Hawkchurch a fair in 1459 which was held in the avenue of lime trees leading to the house.

The Cotley Harriers at the Hunters Lodge Inn in 1911. This really was once a lodge for huntsmen but stories that it was a coaching inn are untrue. The Crewkerne Road opposite was not cut until the nineteenth century, and traffic from Uplyme and Lyme Regis joined the coaching route at Green Lane Cross, half a mile up the road, until quite late in the same century. At best, therefore, it might have been a 'stop' for the odd local using the London–West Country coaches. With the George at Axminster a 'main-line' coaching stopping point, Hunters Lodge would not even have been useful as a place to change horses.

Two

Axminster

Cloakham Bridge, Axminster, with Cloakham House in the background, *c.* 1902.

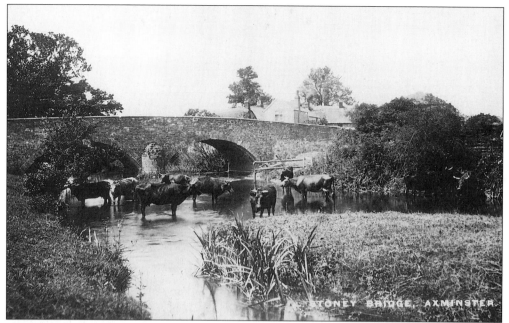

Stoney Bridge, Axminster, *c.* 1906, where the Membury road crosses the Axe as it loops to the north of the town.

Bow Bridge, Axminster, *c.* 1910. Billy Bow lived in Kilmington and made a living selling an antidote to snake bites. His pitch involved taking an adder from a sack and letting it bite him, then taking a liberal swig from a bottle of Bow's Snake Bite Cure and so surviving. One day at Axminster Market, having received the customary bite, he found he had left his medicine behind at Kilmington. He rushed home to get some but, driven mad by the poison, he jumped off the bridge that bears his name to this day. And if you believe that old story you would have believed Billy Bow's claims for his medicine!

16

The River Yarty, seen here in around 1910 at its junction with its parent river between Westwater and Kilmington, is the River Axe's largest tributary.

Axminster photographer Charles Humphries catches the Axe in around 1914 in one of its all-too-frequent winterish moments below the railway station, an area prone to flooding.

Hakes Buildings (later Hillhead Terrace), Musbury Road, Axminster, *c.* 1910.

The Wesleyan Chapel, Lyme Street, Axminster, *c.* 1920. Axminster's first Wesleyan meeting place was situated on the corner end of South Street, and John Wesley contributed to its building fund. He visited the town at least twice afterwards and preached in the Market Place. This chapel was destroyed and, for a time, services were held in the Congregational Chapel. A new chapel was opened in 1796 next to the Market Place. After the chapel seen here was opened in 1894, the old chapel was used by lace-makers.

North Street and the cricket field, Axminster, *c.* 1908. The cricket club was formed in 1874 and occupied the North Street ground for over 100 years before moving to its present Cloakham home at the start of the 1988 season.

Millbrook Hill, Axminster, *c.* 1902. This is the Roman Fosse Way which runs up Stoney Lane, where the photographer was standing, and heads for the sea at Seaton. George Pulman, like far too many Victorian historians, mistakenly takes the Fosse into Axminster. The cottages on the left were demolished some time after the Second World War. The Mill Brook, a tributary of the Axe, takes its name from the old mill out of sight on the right. It was the manor mill for Prestaller. The owner of Weycroft Hall enjoyed the right to have his corn ground there free of charge.

Oak House School, Chard Street, Axminster, c. 1905. In later years the school became the offices of Axminster RDC and it is now a retirement home.

Some of the school's pupils in 1912. Back row, left to right: Alan Beasley, ? Dunn, John Dare, John Snell, Tom Mayo, Dick Harris, Owen Manley, George Warren, Eddie Sanders, Fred Hallett, Mr Thomas Ramsay (principal). Front: Leslie Morrish, Cecil Gage, Jack Newbery, ? Bond, Leonard Newbery, -?-, T. Millard.

Axminster Great Market, 12 May 1904. Granted in the reign of King John, the weekly market was held for centuries in the square and the adjoining streets. Increased traffic led to the market's being moved to its present home off South Street in 1912. And just as well. Imagine the modern-day traffic trying to thread its way through this little lot! Below is a view of the 'new' market not many weeks after it opened in 1912.

Edwin Dawkins' Boot Factory, Chard Street, Axminster, c. 1930. The buildings were severely damaged by incendiary bombs during an air raid on the night of 27-28 February 1942, when some fifty incendiaries fell on the school next door. The boot factory was later demolished.

A Charles Humphries photograph of extension work to Axminster Secondary School in around 1910. Dawkins Boot Factory can be seen in the background.

Mr Cornish (with glasses), the President of the Hospital Committee, lays the foundation stone of Axminster Cottage Hospital in Chard Street on 6 September 1911. The hospital had been situated in the old carpet factory buildings in Silver Street since 1886 and was largely the work of Mrs Emily Conybeare Craven, seen below (in front of the second left window) at the new hospital's official opening on 18 June 1912.

The County Council Schools, Axminster, c. 1905.

Axminster's steam-operated fire engine outside the fire station in West Street in around 1905. The horses were hired from the stables at the Old Bell Hotel some 200 yards back down the road, which must have added to the time it took to get the fireman on the road and racing off to the fire. It is almost certain that this picture is of the horses being harnessed prior to the engine's departure for a fire. Otherwise there would hardly be such a crowd of spectators or two long arms of Axminster's law keeping a watchful eye on the proceedings. The building behind provides an interesting glimpse into Axminster's past. On the extreme left is the entrance to some houses that stood back from the road; Peter Peach's barbers shop can be found there today. Next to it is George Parsons' coach-building workshop; this later became Collards jewellers shop, and is now an antique shop. Then comes the fire station, which is now the Curtain Gallery, followed by a harness makers business, which later became Trivett's radio and TV shop and now their toy shop. (Owner Bert Trivett has worked there for the past fifty years.) Then came Mr Mearing's shop, now the Alliance and Leicester, and Snell's printing works, later the TSB but now closed.

Axminster station, *c.* 1870. The railway arrived at Axminster on 18 July 1860, but only after a lengthy debate over which route the line from London, via Salisbury, to Exeter would run. Happily for Axminster, the so-called 'middle' route was chosen. Equally happily, just over a century later, the infamous Beeching Axe spared the station.

Newenham Abbey, Axminster, seen here in a mid-nineteenth century drawing, was founded in 1247 in the lush water meadows to the south-west of the town by William Brewer, the second son of Lord Brewer. A Cistercian abbey, it was first peopled by an abbot, twelve choir-monks and four lay-brothers from the existing community at Beaulieu who walked from there to Axminster. It fell foul of Henry VIII's Dissolution (1539) and much of its vast estates were leased to Sir Henry Grey, Marquess of Dorset. After his execution and attainder for the part he played in the coup that attempted to put his daughter, Lady Jane Grey, on the throne, the property reverted to the Throne and was later granted by Elizabeth I to Thomas, Duke of Norfolk. It was sold to the Petre family and remained in their hands for over 200 years (1605-1824). Today just a few crumbling stones are all that remain of the abbey.

The original Green Dragon Inn at the foot of Castle Hill, Axminster, in around 1875. George Heal was landlord when this photograph was taken by a Mr J.M. Newbery of Axminster. And it was the same George Heal who had established the nearby Iron Foundry in 1876. Most of the foundry, sold to H. Norrington & Son Ltd of Exeter in 1921, still stands. Sadly, however, the Green Dragon closed in 1971.

The George Hotel, Axminster, c. 1880. Cromwell's men stayed at the George during the Civil War, and at the height of the coaching era as many as eighteen coaches used it daily. The present building is of the eighteenth century. Note the narrowness of Lyme Street at the time. The advent of the motor car led to the George's losing the rooms seen here on the right. During the street widening an Adam fireplace was removed from the original dining room and put in an upstairs room.

JAMES SMYTH,

ESTABLISHED 1710.

Agent for the
Sun, Fire and Life, Offices,

Family Grocer,
Italian Warehouseman,
and ✎✎
Provision Merchant.

DEALER
IN
WINES,
ALE, ✎
AND
PORTER.
✎

Finest Wiltshire Bacon.
Cheddar, Stilton, and Fancy Cheese
from selected makers.
Crosse & Blackwell's Pickles,
Sauces and Condiments.
Huntley & Palmer's
Celebrated Reading Biscuits.

Wholesale and Retail
Grain and
Fodder Merchant.
❦❦❦

Lyme Street and
South Street,

AXMINSTER.

Smyth's grocery shop on the corner of Lyme Street and South Street, Axminster, c. 1903. One of Axminster's oldest businesses, it was established in 1710, taken over by a Mr Sheppard soon after this picture was taken, and then bought by a Mr Webber. Today the site is the South Street car park.

Parsons coach builders in West Street, Axminster in around 1912. Of interest is the advertisement above the door which says they 'upholster and paint motor cars'. They have made a first class job of the one seen here!

27

Axminster Square, *c*. 1922. In an age when traffic was not a problem on the main road through the town, the buses waited in the Square rather than on the road.

Weycroft Mills, Axminster, seen here in around 1908, was a working mill until the 1970s but allowed to fall into complete (and sad) disrepair. It has just been sold and will, hopefully, be redeveloped. Three generations of the Morrish family owned the mill. Although the present building is thought to be Victorian, there has been a mill here since Domesday. This building was a flour mill, its two stones driven by two water turbines which were sometimes supplemented by power from a small diesel engine. According to George Pulman there was an inn close by called 'The Sine of the Sammon' in the very early years of the nineteenth century.

Three
Kilmington, Whitford and Musbury

The Cross and the Old Inn, Kilmington, *c.* 1912.

The Old Inn, Kilmington, *c.* 1904. Note the narrowness of the now busy A35 part of the Folkestone-Honiton trunk road in this and the lower picture. It was once the Roman road linking Durnovarian (Dorchester) and Isca (Exeter) crossing the original Fosse Way at the top of Stoney Lane in Axminster.

The Axe Vale Harriers meet outside the inn at around the same time.

St Giles' church, Kilmington, in 1902.

St Giles' church, Kilmington, c. 1903. This is obviously something other than an ordinary Sunday service if the 'Sunday-best' turn-out is anything to go by.

French Brothers' Bakery, Kilmington, *c.* 1899. Alice French is standing on the old Roman road as it climbs away to Shute Woods and Isca (Exeter). Kilmington Chapel is just off the picture to the left. Deliveries at this time would have been by horse and cart.

French's later joined the motor age with this Model T Ford.

The Street, Kilmington, *c.* 1895.

The Green and the post office, Kilmington, *c.* 1908.

Mr Youlden ran a store at Colyton. Judging by the cans on his waggon, seen here at Shute Pillars in around 1905, he also delivered paraffin to the nearby villages.

Seaton Junction, *c.* 1920.

Shute House, once the home of the Bonvilles and then the Poles, was originally built in 1380 by Sir William Bonville. It was rebuilt and all that remains of the old house is the castellated gatehouse (above), which dates from around 1550, and one wing (below). Both are seen here in 1900. The Pole family rented Shute from around the middle of the sixteenth century until 1787, when they bought the estate and built the new Shute House. They used much of the stone from the older house. In later years the newer building became a girls' school and has now been turned into flats.

The tiny brick church of St Mary's at Whitford during its construction in 1910. It has seating for just thirty-six people.

Seaton Junction station in 1888, just after the Shute Arms Hotel was built and its gardens freshly planted out. The Seaton & Beer Railway Company got the go-ahead for a branch line to Seaton in 1863 and the line opened for business on 16 March 1868. When diesel services were introduced in 1963 the end was already in sight, Beeching's infamous 'axe' closing the line on 7 March 1966. Seaton Junction was built in 1860 after the main Waterloo line had been extended westward from Salisbury but it was originally called Colyton (for Seaton). After the branch line closed the junction was used for just over a year for loading milk from the local milk factory run by Express Dairies.

Whitford, *c.* 1910, with the Methodist chapel in the background.

Whitford, *c.* 1910. George Pulman claims that the name of the village comes from 'wide ford' and evens hints at a connection with 'White-friars-ford'. The river is not noticeably wide at this point, however, and in all probability the connection is with 'white ford'. The Axe glistens milky white where it runs over the stones at the old ford near Whitford Bridge.

The Hare & Hounds and Whitford village, *c.* 1907.

Whitford outing. Pump Farm, Whitford, seen here in the early 1930s, is of fifteenth-century origin and has been farmed by the Loud family for some 400 years. Family records indicate that is has been called Pump Farm for at least 300 years, which suggests it once gave the village at least some of its water supplies. The sign post and village green are no longer with us.

The first Whitford Bridge, seen here around the turn of the century, was a foot bridge, wheeled traffic and herded cattle still using the old ford. The advent of the motor age, however, led to the building of the second bridge (below) before the First World War. Built of iron, it was single-carriageway and proved to be far too narrow for anything much wider than a car; there were few double-decker buses on the Seaton–Taunton run that did not carry scrape marks collected as they crossed it. A wider, perhaps more handsome but certainly not more interesting, bridge takes the traffic over the Axe today. It was built in 1976 at a cost of £232,000.

The toll house between Whitford and Musbury, seen here in around 1905, was once part of the Axminster Turnpike Trust, whose terms and conditions (laid down in 1822) included fines for playing football, scalding meat, stopping others from passing, and letting gates swing outward on to the roads concerned.

Chapel Street, Musbury, c. 1906. The chapel is seen in the background. George Pulman said of it, 'There is a dissenting place of worship in the village, erected in 1859, but not, I believe, in connection with any denomination.'

Axminster Road, Musbury, *c.* 1910, before the new (Marlborough) road was cut.

The post office, Musbury, *c.* 1903. This view conjures up George Pulman's vision of the village when, according to him, it was 'a pretty specimen of an English village – with its ancient church, its squire's mansion, its ale house, where the sheets are "smelling of lavender", and its detached cottages in the midst of flower gardens – forming a congenial resting-place, in the evening of life, for the lover of nature, of angling, and of rural retirement.' It still is.

Wisteria Cottage, Musbury, *c.* 1904.

Combpyne Road, Musbury, *c.* 1903. Musbury takes its name from the late Iron Age fortress that broods over the village from the hill behind it. The Saxons are said to have found the fort over-run with mice when they arrived at the start of the seventh century and called it 'mus burh' (OE) – literally 'mouse fort'. It appears in Domesday as 'Musberia'.

Fore Street, Musbury, *c.* 1920. The bakers shop on the left was once run by Tommy Bennett, then by George Seward. The bakery and shop closed in the 1950s, when a Mr Reed was the baker. Below is the same view but from the opposite direction.

Ashe House, Musbury, seen above soon after the turn of the century, came into the hands of the Drake family when John Drake, one of the auditors during the suppression of nearby Newenham Abbey, purchased it. His great grand-daughter Elizabeth married a Dorset knight called Winston Churchill and in 1650 gave him a son, another John, who grew up to become the famous military leader, the Duke of Marlborough. Some doubt exists as to whether he was born at Ashe, which was burnt by the Royalists during the Civil War, or the nearby farmhouse at Trill (below), which belonged to the family. But Musbury's St Michael's parish church proudly displays the facsimile of the entry from the parish register and Ashe is in Musbury parish and Trill in Axminster. That facsimile also clears up the mystery over his date of birth, which his descendant Winston Churchill gives as 26 June (actually his date of baptism) in his *Marlborough*, and as 'May or June' in his *History of the English Speaking People*. George Pulman got it mixed up as well. He gives 24 June as the birth date and then quotes the Axminster registers which give 18 June, six days earlier, as his baptismal day! He was born on 26th May.

Four
Colyton and Colyford

The East Devon Hunt outside the Globe Inn, Colyton, c. 1908. Now the Kingfisher, the Globe was an old established Colyton inn, its name, according to George Pulman, was 'the favourite [sic] emblem of outfitter trade and others who rely upon cosmopolitan customers'. The shop behind the Globe was Mrs Porter's grocery shop.

Firemen fighting the flames at Colyton's St Andrew's church in 1933, when most of the interior was gutted and the nave and south aisle left open to the skies. Happily, the church, among the best parish churches in Devon, was left in possibly better condition by the restorers. As if to prove the old adage about an ill wind, some oddly carved stones discovered embedded in the tower during the restoration proved to be one of the earliest Saxon crosses in Devon and are thought to date at least from Alfred's reign. The present St Andrew's dates from Norman times, the east end of the chancel and the central crossing tower being of this period; the chancel itself dates from 1383.

The interior of St Andrew's church, Colyton, c. 1928. The Ten Commandments above the arch at the end of the nave were not restored after the 1933 fire. The pair of magnificent chandeliers seen here cost £80 when purchased in 1796. They hold thirty-six candles each and, fortunately, did survive the fire.

Ern Bastable's bakers shop, Vicarage Street, Colyton, *c.* 1920. The popular baker and civic person later made his deliveries with the Model T Ford seen below. It is interesting to note in the top picture that Colyton Police Station was in Vicarage Street.

Colyton Industrial & Providential Society, Sidmouth Road, Colyton, c. 1920. The staff are, left to right: Donald Purse, Mr Jay (manager), Irene Restorick, Roy French, Norman Bishop, Harold Purse. The Co-op baked its own bread on the premises at the time and had done so for many years, as evidenced by the unknown delivery boy posing below during his rounds about 1909.

Girls' Group II, Colyton School, c. 1906.

Colyton Football Club, 1924-25. The club won the coveted Morrison Bell Cup when they beat Budleigh Salterton 1-0 with a Fry goal at Honiton after a 1-1 draw (also at Honiton). On the team's return to Colyton it was met at the Green Bridge by Colyton Ex-Servicemen's Band and escorted to the club's HQ at Colyton Men's Institute. Earlier they had beaten Seaton 2-0 in the first ever final of the Lyme Hospital Cup. But Colyton had also finished bottom of the Perry Street League, and only ten weeks later the club disbanded through lack of support. The team and officers here are, back row, left to right: George White, Reg White, -?-, Bill Solway, Donald Baker, ? Jarvis, -?-, -?-, -?-. Middle: Charlie Facey, Bert Warren, Harry Strawbridge (chairman), Ern Bastable, -?-. Front: Bert Copp, George Fry, Billy Hann, -?-.

The Gerrard Arms, Colyton, *c.* 1900, with White's butchers shop to the right.

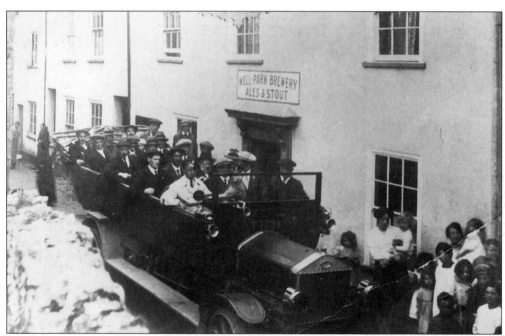

Lower Church Street (then Cross Street) in the early 1920s. It is not known whether the all-male party on the charabanc are regulars at the George Inn or at St Andrew's church, out of sight on the other side of the road.

Colombe Garage, Colyton, *c.* 1938. Today the site is a car park. Left to right: Perce Trivett, Tommy Butler, -?-, Arthur Phare.

Colyton Fair, 1907. The lady second right is Laura-Lee Newton. Colyton Fair was granted by King John. In 1342 a Peter de Browse was granted a market, but by the time of the above picture that had virtually ceased to exist, and the fair followed soon after.

Hillhead Road, Colyton, *c.* 1900.

South Street, Colyton, *c.* 1908. The long since closed Compasses Inn is on the left. The thatched building on the right comprising a private dwelling and Ern Tolman's cycle shop (with the bicycles outside) was later demolished to widen the entrance to Market Place and the Square. Today Colyton library stands on part of the site.

Colyton fire station and engine, *c.* 1910.

Soup Day, Colyton, *c.* 1900. The Feoffees of Colyton held a weekly soup kitchen at the town lock-up (behind). It was aimed at the poor and needy but one wonders how 'poor and needy' some of the children seen here really were! The Feoffees had founded Colyton Grammar School in 1546. Other services they provided included a town leat (1647) which brought water down from springs near Ridgeway until 1893, when a piped supply replaced it. In 1858 they provided the town's lighting using naphtha lamps, in 1927 the Feoffees Town Hall, and down the years they had been to the forefront in providing clothing, fuel and food to those in need.

The Market Place, Colyton, in the late nineteenth century. The row of mostly thatched buildings on the left have gone. The extreme left hand building, now Lloyds Bank, was the Dolphin Inn.

Coronation Day, Colyton, 1911. The children of the town are apparently off for a ride to allow the tables on the left to be loaded with food.

Laying the foundation stone of the Feoffees Hall in Colyton Square in 1926. Among those seen are Sammy Hooper and Ern Bastaple. Hooper (in front in the cap) was a mason and the foreman for the Colyton building firm of Richards who built the Hall.

Board's grocery shop, Queen Street, Colyton, *c.* 1905.

The Colyton draper A. Symons & Co was well known for its Christmas displays such as that seen here in around 1930. The men's department was behind the smaller window on the right; the rest of the ground floor was given up to the gentler sex, who probably also had more than their fair share of the upstairs hat department. Symonds were certainly there in the 1890s (they can be seen in the picture below in 1896), and they continued to trade at London House until the 1950s.

Perhaps the old horse would not have died on the way home from Widdecombe Fair if it had had the use of the Devon County Council steam lorry used here for the 'Old Uncle Tom Cobbley' tableau in the 1927 Colyton Carnival.

Colyton Fair, *c.* 1910. Colyton was granted a fair in 1208 by King John, and rights for a market are said to have been given to a Peter de Browse around 1342 in the reign of Edward III. *Pulman's Weekly News* said of the latter in 1890 that 'To business men, Colyton market has never presented much of an attraction. Tuesday's was a complete failure with only a handful of stock – mainly pigs. They have degenerated into pleasurable occasions utilised by the younger generation for the disposal of pence they might have spent to greater advantage.' This picture of sheep penned outside the Colcombe Castle in the Square in 1907 hardly supports this pessimistic view.

Colyton fair was not just about selling livestock. It gave the fair sex the chance to parade in their Sunday best, as here in 1908.

The Axe Vale Harriers at the entrance to Colcombe Farm, Colyton, around 1903.

R. Woran's saddler's shop and newsagents, East Street, Colyton. The picture can be dated to the turn of the century thanks to the *Pulman's Weekly News* contents bill on the left which tells of 'Great Battles ... British Victorious ... Heavy Boer Losses.'

Quite by coincidence, this picture, dated 1906 and showing a Mr W.E. Davis now the saddler and shopkeeper, was posted to Port Elizabeth, South Africa!

The 'Wayside Tent' Service in a field beside the River Coly at Green Bridge, Colyton, *c.* 1902. Shiphay Farm is in the background.

Colyton Swimming Pool, seen here in around 1918, was a gift to the town by Sir Frederick de la Pole of Shute House in 1914. It cost £200 and was built beside the Shute Stream near Horse Lane Road. Made with concrete sides and bottom and measuring some sixty by twenty-five feet, it drew water from the Umborne rather than the nearer, and reputedly dirtier, Coly. The flushing pipe ran five hundred yards to a drain. Sir Frederick opened the pool on 2 August 1914, the ceremony ironically taking place in the School House (Colyton Grammar School) because it was raining! Welcoming Sir Frederick, the chairman of the Feoffees, Mr F. Follett, told all the boys to learn to swim 'in order to lead clean and healthy lives'.

The junction of the Umborne Brook and the River Coly just outside Colyton. The turnpike gate once stood near here, where the road from Axminster crosses the Coly via the Umborne Bridge. The bridge, once a narrow pack horse type, was widened in the middle of the nineteenth century. In the background is a smithy with Stokes Butter Factory behind it. The butter factory later moved to Chard Junction.

The White Hart, Church Street, Colyton, c. 1864, in one of the oldest known pictures of Colyton. Taken by W.H. Hamilton Rogers FSA, the original was given by George Eyre-Evans in 1922 to the landlord of the White Hart, Mr Rendell.

A drawing (*c.* 1860) of James Abraham's drapers shop in Queen Square, Colyton. This later became the Liberty Cycle Shop.

The Liberty Cycle Shop, Queen Square, Colyton, seen here in around 1905, was run by the Richards brothers. S.J. Soanes Ltd later took over the premises and cycles have now been sold from the same place for nearly 100 years. Of special interest here are the motor cycles, however. The one on the right, which is unregistered, is probably a Bowden; on the left is a 1905 500cc Ariel with the Devon number T373.

S.J. Soanes' Garage, Queen Square, Colyton, *c.* 1935. Left to right: Harold Colson, Charlie Facey, Edgar Smith. Syd Soanes took over the business in around 1926, his son Frank ran it from 1949 to 1973, and the premises remain in the family's hands today.

Sidmouth Street, Colyton, *c.* 1906. Mr Copp's blacksmiths shop is the background.

The Lion Inn, Colyton, seen here at the turn of the century, was severely damaged by fire in around 1909 (below) and never re-opened. It stood on the corner of West Street and King Street and today is the site of Devonshire Terrace.

Bill and Fred Copp were blacksmiths in West Street, Colyton. The smithy, seen here in around 1908, was severely damaged by fire during the 1930s but the brothers continued in business until after the Second World War and the premises are still there.

Looking into Queen Square from Church Street, Colyton, c. 1890. Colyton Cottage in the background, probably the best of Colyton's many lovely houses, was built around the end of the sixteenth century. Inside, over a bedroom fireplace, are the date and initials '1610 EVMV' and the text, 'Who so feareth the Lord shall prosper and in the date of his end shall be blessed.'

Fred Abrahams's tailors shop in Colyton Square around 1901. Mr Abrahams is in the middle and his wife on the right with their daughter Kathleen. Today the premises is a jewellers shop.

Colyton Grammar School, 1908, shortly before the headmaster Mr Mermagen (seated centre with his wife on his left) left to take up a similar post at Ilminster Grammar School. Colyton Grammar School was founded in 1546 when the Feoffees of the town bought back some of the lands of Henry Courtenay, Marquis of Exeter, who had been executed on a trumped-up charge of treason on the orders of Henry VIII. They used some of the income from those lands to endow the school for 'the goodly and virtuous education of children in Colyton for ever'. Today, 450 years later and in its fourth home at Gully Shute near Colyford, Colyton Grammar School continues to live up to those words.

Colyton's committee to arrange the festivities for Queen Victoria's Diamond Jubilee in 1897.

Colyton bell-ringers, *c.* 1934. Back row, left to right: Dick Barrett, Fred Dart, Jack Bowles, Bill Hussey, Gordon Snell, Stan Moss, Revd Wyatt. Front: Jim Newbery, Ned Moss, Jim Summers, Billy Bowles.

Swan Hill, Colyford, *c.* 1905. The low shed at right angles to the road in this and the lower picture was the workshop of local wheelwright and carpenter Mr Langford who was said to have drawn the curtains when he was making a coffin. Today, of course, the building is the bar of the appropriately named Wheelwright pub.

The village centre, looking the other way.

Colyford, *c.* 1908.

Colyford, looking east, *c.* 1900. Both the high wall on the left and the house behind it have been demolished. According to George Pulman, the bridge, barely visible behind the cyclist, which now takes the Roman road over the River Coly and into the village, was erected around 1830 upon the site of an older bridge, upon which was cut the date 1681.

The salmon trap on the River Axe between Axe Bridge and Axmouth in 1963 when the river froze over. The trap was used to catch and tag salmon entering and leaving the river but is no longer there.

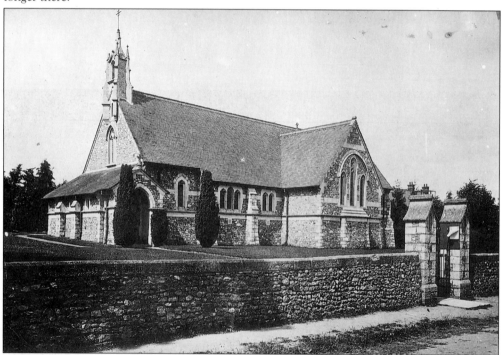

St Michael's church, Colyford, c. 1921. St Michael's was built as recently as 1888 by John Scarborough who, the story says, worshipped at St Andrew's in Colyton with the rest of the family until he had a violent row with a brother. Vowing never to worship under the same roof as the brother ever again, he built the tiny church at Colyford. He would hardly have been pleased when, in later years, St Michael's became a chapel-of-ease to St Andrew's. Scarborough was also responsible for closing a pub called the Swan which he owned. Workmen building a new house for him were absent when he called in at the site. He found them close by in the Swan and, after sacking the lot, closed the place.

Five

Seaton

The proclamation of King George V in Seaton Square on 9 May 1910. Every eye, except those of the dog in the left foreground, is on the stage from where the proclamation is being read. Of interest are the overdone advertisements on the West London Tobacco Stores (now the Midland Bank) and Baker's grocery shop (now Somerfields), a business name retained there until after the Second World War.

Castle Hill, Seaton, from a James Townsend drawing in 1882. Townsend calls this 'SEATON, DEVON. THE BATHS'; in fact the Bath House is not in the top picture but it can be seen below in another James drawing. It is the central building behind the horseman. This view, looking down Castle Hill, has been a favourite with postcard photographers ever since.

Thomas Clapp, Beach Hotel Mews, Station Road, Seaton, 1902. The Omnibus, Carriage, Posting and Livery Stables firm also had an office in Cross Street which they kept until recent years. Later their stables (and in turn garages) moved to Clapp's Lane, opposite the junction of Manor Road and Fore Street. Like all such local firms, Clapp's sent 'Omnibuses to and from the station to meet every train' and most of their fleet seems to have turned up there in the bottom picture. They specialised in weddings and funerals and were proud of the fact that they could 'always send a Private Omnibus on receipt of wire or letter'.

A 1924 Lancia charabanc outside Arthur Good's Seaton Motor Co. in Station (now Harbour) Road in 1928. Arthur Good is the middle of the five men in the background. His premises were to become Seaton's Southern National Bus Depot. Today it is Surewear.

Clapp's Garage, Clapps Lane, Seaton, *c.* 1928. Although the age of the motor car was well under way when this photograph was taken, Clapp's still used their horse-drawn hearse and, judging by its well-maintained appearance, their horse-drawn bus still 'met every train'.

Seaton station, *c.* 1906.

Seaton station, *c.* 1939. The Seaton branch line was opened on 17 March 1868 and, according to George Pulman, 'has been the means of converting Seaton from one of the most quiet and isolated of sea-side villages into a modern "watering place" of some pretension and yet, happily, not at the sacrifice of much of the original primitiveness which is its greatest charm'.

Seaton station, looking south towards Trevelyan Road, in around 1912.

The staff at Seaton station in around 1908.

The Kings Arms Inn, Fore Street, Seaton, *c.* 1900 when its landlord was a Mr Salter. The lower picture was taken towards the end of the 1930s when Arthur Hooper was landlord. Although reputed to be an old coaching inn (bay windows in hotels often indicate this; passengers could sit and watch for their coach here), there is no side entrance in the earlier picture. At the time of the later picture this led to what the landlord called the stables. In the second picture the door has moved to the right to take the place of the old window.

Overmass & Chapple's coach maker's yard, off Sidmouth Street, c. 1900. Orders are being carried out for the well-known Seaton butchering family of J.H. Loud and for Pearce the builder, whose cart bears the date 1901.

Although this picture from the 1903 edition of *The Axe Valley Illustrated* in the *Mate's Illustrated Guides* series is described as Seaton Tennis Ground, and tennis is obviously being played here, it is in fact the Cricket Field seen from the main gate. Eyewell Green, Townsend and Meadow Avenue, all of which would be plainly visible in the background today, are not even twinkles in the developer's eye at this time.

Old Beer Road, Seaton, in the 1920s. Given the steepness of the hills between Seaton and Beer, especially the old and steep Beer Hill just out of sight at the bottom of this picture, it is not surprising that this load of Beer stone on its way to Seaton railway station needs two horses to pull it. Compare the width of the road and pavement here with today's road which has been considerably narrowed by the many mini-landslips the cliffs are prone to at this point.

Seaton Red Cross was formed in 1916 when the late Maud Holmes (second left in the front row), a member of the Axminster detachment, was asked to form a detachment in Seaton for staffing at Ryall's Court. A matron and two sisters were appointed and, with the help of Seaton members who had been enrolled and trained, the hospital was soon ready for the first arrival of the wounded soldiers. Between the two wars membership fluctuated, but Devon 110, as it was known, continued to work in the district. It was to give outstanding service to the town during the Second World War and continues to do so to this day.

Gage's East Devon Supply Stores, Fore Street, Seaton, *c.* 1901. Gage was a general grocer, provision, wine, spirit and ale merchant. Later, the business, including a small branch at Beer, was bought by the Sidmouth-based Trumps firm and is today a Co-op branch.

Gould & Son's Cross Street Machine Bakery, on the corner of Cross Street and Fore Street. Established as early as 1832, Gould's had just had a complete refit when this picture was taken in 1902. He 'begged to call the attention of Visitors and Residents of the District to their UP-TO-DATE BAKERY, fitted with the LATEST MACHINERY for the manufacture of Bread, etc, under the most scientific principles and best Hygienic conditions'. Gould's was later taken over by Benny Selway, and then George Rowe, both of whom kept up Gould's high standards.

Lower Fore Street, Seaton, *c.* 1906.

Probably one of the oldest photographs of Seaton's Fore Street in existence and dating from before 1875. Today Akerman's ironmongers shop is on the extreme left where the buildings, apart from the introduction of shop fronts, have not changed all that much. It is a different story on the right, however, where the row of houses bears little comparison with today's scene.

Upper Fore Street, Seaton, *c.* 1899.

One of the beauties of the Dawlish-based postcard firm of Chapman and Son was that it wandered into the back streets and took pictures there, and in so doing unwittingly rendered great service to later local historians. They frequently accepted orders for as few as twenty-five cards, especially from hotels who would then sell the cards to guests. This view of the Pole Arms in Seaton's Fore Street in 1909 is probably part of one such order. Note the continuous iron fencing on the left, much of which vanished during salvage drives in the Second World War.

Queen Street, Seaton, *c.* 1899.

Mutter & Sons Fish Shop, Queen Street, Seaton, in the 1920s. The family had begun selling fish from a small shop situated where Bernard Pitt's chemists shop can be found today. Edgar Augustus Mutter bought the premises seen here in 1919 after service in the First World War and opened the shop the following year. He is seen outside in the mid-1920s with his wife Elizabeth Ann. The shop stayed in the family's hands until 1976. Since then it has been run by Fred Cockram, who started work there as an errand boy at the age of twelve and now, fifty-one years later, is the boss.

F.W. Thomas's Seaton Farm Dairy on the corner of Sidmouth Street and Cross Street, *c.* 1905. Mr Thomas delivered twice daily throughout Seaton using the milk float seen here.

Sidmouth Street, Seaton, some years before the turn of the century. In later years these old thatched cottages disappeared and the Auto Service showrooms and the Avenue appeared on the right end. The others, after being rebuilt and losing their front gardens, were, one-by-one, converted into shops.

Friedenheim Seaside School for Girls, c. 1880, possibly while it was still a private house. It later became known as Montpellier Girls' School and enjoyed a high reputation, especially with the children of Anglo-Indians, at the turn of the century, when a Miss Mary Grover was the principal. She was 'assisted by five resident mistresses and visiting masters' who prepared the children for the Junior and Senior Cambridge and London Matriculation and also for advanced examinations in music (London R.A.M.). With 'bathing, hockey, and all healthy physical exercises encouraged', it is hardly surprising that the school's motto was *Mens sana in corpore sano* ('a Healthy Mind in a Healthy Body'). The ivy-clad building to the left of the school later became part of Ferris & Prescott's drapery and is now Seaton's new police station.

Manor Cottages, Seaton, *c.* 1909, then the virtual end of the town.

Seaton Square, looking into Fore Street, *c.* 1922.

W.J. Agland & Co., Marine Place, Seaton, *c.* 1899. Agland's premises, then an outfitters and drapers, is now the site of the offices of Milford & Dormer, the solicitors.

Seaton postal staff outside the post office in around 1899. The lady on the left is Mrs Florrie Gush; the lady third from the left is Mrs Elizabeth Akerman, the postmistress and a member of the family (Akerman) that provided Seaton's postmaster or mistress for most of the nineteenth century. William Miller is the postman on the right.

The Square, Seaton, c. 1910. This view looking into Marine Place and towards the sea was, for reasons unknown, not popular with postcard photographers.

C.F. Gosney, The Pharmacy, Marine Crescent, Seaton. Gosney believed in the power of advertising and was not modest with it either. With this picture, taken from a 1903 advert, he states 'Physicians Prescriptions Accurately Dispensed ... Gosney's Bronchial Syrup, a Safe and Efficacious Cure for Coughs, Colds, Bronchitis, Difficulty of Breathing, etc ... Gosney's Neuralgic Mixture, an Infallible Remedy (bottles 1/6d) ... Gosney's Extra Cream Skin Soap, Unequalled for the Complexion and Delicate Skins (4d each) ... Drugs and Chemicals of the Purest Quality ... and Compound Benzoin Lotion, an invaluable preparation for the prevention of Freckles, and the removal of Redness and Roughness caused by the the Sun or Wind. For the Complexion it stands unrivalled.' (The Victorian belief that sunburnt looks were not ladylike obviously persisted.)

Seaton front, c. 1908.

Tommy Sloman ran posting and livery stables in Seaton's Fore Street and Station (now Harbour) Road. The Fore Street stables (right) were next to the Pole Arms Hotel, from where Sloman operated a horse-drawn omnibus service (below) that met all trains and charged a 3d fare to and from the station for all parts of the town, without luggage. Among the many other services he advertised were 'carriages of every description ... three-horse brake ... saddle horses ... lessons in riding and driving ... horses broken to saddle, harness, jumping, etc, etc, ... horses taken in livery and bait'.

Royal Clarence Hotel, on the corner of Station Road and Marine Crescent, Seaton. Seen here in 1902, it claimed to be 'within a ten-minute walk of the splendid Axe Cliff Gold Links' (which is pushing it a bit!). It was built in 1866, probably to meet the influx of visitors expected in two years time, when the railway was due to reach Seaton.

The picture below, taken after a blizzard, is of a much earlier date, probably even before 1880. The cottages on the left were demolished well before the turn of the century and replaced by a row of mostly three-storey replacements. An older building stands at the top of Station (now Harbour) Road, where Gould's Restaurant (see opposite) had appeared by the turn of the century.

Gould's Temperance Hotel and Restaurant, at the corner of Station Road and The Square, where Woolworths stands today.

Seaton sea front, looking towards Marine Crescent and the town, in around 1902. The granite drinking fountain, in the centre of the picture, which celebrated Queen Victoria's Diamond Jubilee in 1897, was the gift of the family of Mr W.H. Willans, long resident in Seaton. It was finally demolished some years after the Second World War in the interests of traffic movement. The flag on the right flew from the roof of Gould's Hotel and Restaurant (above) on the corner of Station Road. The building in the left foreground is Seaton Bath House, the last of three such buildings there; it was demolished soon after this picture was taken.

Seaton, *c.* 1899. Note the number of fishing boats on the beach and the way in which the Bath House dominates the now open space at the entrance to Marine Place.

Another of the views of Seaton popular with postcard photographers. Dated around 1900, it is of interest if only for the fact that it shows that the Royal Clarence Hotel was part of the Seaton Beach and Clarence Hotels Company. Critics of Seaton claim that because it developed late as a watering place 'it is full of ugly but interesting Victorian architecture'. There is nothing ugly about the handsome Victorian buildings on the left, although they have probably lost something today, having been turned into shops and offices on the ground floor.

Fred Diment's Garage, Station Road, Seaton, shortly after it opened in 1905. Three years later the business was sold to Benny Trevett and it stayed in his family's hands until the 1970s. Soon after this picture was taken Diment had a second storey added to the shop. R.G. Rodgers' shop on the right dealt in antique furniture and china. It later belonged to Harold Rodgers and became a newsagents selling sweets and toys.

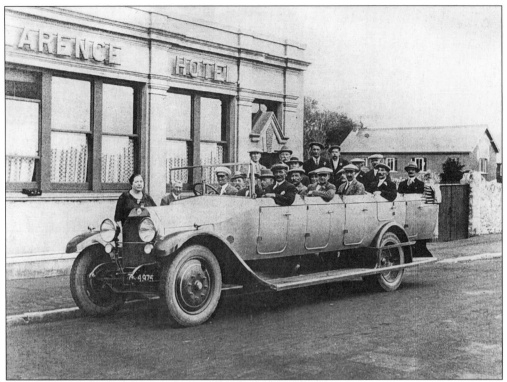

A charabanc outing prepares to leave the Royal Clarence Hotel at the top of Seaton's Station Road in around 1930. The part of the hotel seen here was the public bar but it is now a sports shop.

Seaton sea front, *c.* 1919.

Sunday best on Seaton front in the 1890s. The dark windows in the background are the Seaton branch of Lloyds Bank, which moved to its present home on the corner of Marine Place and Eyre Court Road in the early twentieth century. Around the time of the move, the left-hand part of the building seen here gained the second storey seen in the picture below, which dates from the later 1920s.

Mr Gosney (see p. 88) ought to know better. He published this postcard in the 1920s and called it Violet Terrace. That terrace looked out on to the entrance to the Regal Cinema and vanished with the cinema in 1972. This view is actually of Major Terrace, which runs at right angles to Sidmouth Street.

Another wrongly labelled card. Called Seaton Terrace here, it is Seafield Terrace seen around 1909, when the present bowling green was in fact a field.

The Parade, Seaton, c. 1914. The Westleigh Hotel stands on the extreme right; next to it, on the other side of Seahill Hill, is Seafield, a house destroyed in the Second World War by a stick of bombs dropped from a Junkers 88 in a 'tip-and-run' raid on the town.

The Beach Hotel and the West Walk, Seaton, c. 1925. The Beach was Seaton's leading hotel but after the Second World War it became a County Council Old People's Home known as White Cliff, which was controversially closed a few years ago.

The mouth of the River Axe around the turn of the century, showing development of Station Road and the East Walk only reaching as far as Beach Road. Of interest to the left of the bridge, near the edge of the river, are the walls of the coal yards. The whole of Seaton Marsh was once an arm of the sea and it was from the creek that Seaton's original name of Fleete (OE) sprang. Forced to move nearer the sea when the creek dried out after its mouth became blocked by a wall of shingle, the inhabitants of Fleete arrived at a 'sea-farm' or, again in Old English, a 'sea-tun'. That is how Seaton got its new name.

Six

Beer

Clapp Street, Beer, c. 1907.

Bovey House, *c.* 1914. A mile north-west from Beer, Bovey has a leaden shoot with the date 1592 upon it, but there has been a building here since at least the reign of Henry II (1154-89). There is a 180 ft well with, some 30 ft down, a 10 ft square recess which George Pulman claims is a concealment chamber. A later historian, Seaton's Ernest Burnham, says that it was for the man who was cleaning the well to step into whilst the bucket ran up or down. Local tradition has Charles II hiding in a nearby oak but this is more likely to have grown out of a carving inside depicting the king doing this after the Battle of Worcester. There is no proof that he ever got closer to Beer than Charmouth. Bovey was in the hands of the Walrond family from 1300 until 1786, when it passed by marriage to Lord Rolle. It was empty for a while and it was then that the legend of a headless female ghost arrived. In all probability the story originated from the notorious Beer smuggler Jack Rattenbury, who used the area as a meeting place for his smuggler gang. A ghost would keep prying eyes away.

St Michael's church, Beer, seen here in around 1904, was erected in 1877-78 by Lord Rolle as a chapel-of-ease, Beer's parish church at the time being St Gregory's at Seaton. St Michael's, which became Beer's parish church in 1906, was built of Beer stone at a cost of £8,000 and is in the Decorated style. The tall spire was demolished on safety grounds soon after the Second World War and replaced by a short tower.

The original St Michael's church, Beer, c. 1869. It was a chapel-of-ease to its mother church at Seaton, as was the church that replaced it in 1877 (see above). Beer remained under Seaton's vicar until 1905, when the two parishes were separated.

Shepherds Cottage, Beer, *c.* 1902. It is said that as many as five shepherds (from whom the cottage takes its name) lived here at one time.

Although in a museum in Malta and thought to date from the mid-nineteenth century, and even allowing for the artistic licence which brings the sea some five hundred yards up the road and changes the site of the water conduit, this painting has to be of the cottage shown above.

The limestone at Beer, which has been quarried since Roman times, was deposited at the bottom of the sea some 120 million years ago. The 13 ft seam is soft enough to be cut by a handsaw but soon hardens on exposure to air. Most of Exeter Cathedral was built of it and it can be found as far from Devon as St Paul's Cathedral, Westminster, Winchester Cathedral and Rochester. There is hardly a church in East Devon without some of the stone somewhere and many of them are almost entirely constructed of it. In 1900 horses were used to drag the stone out and carry it to Seaton station (see p.79). By 1920 (below) a new kind of 'horsepower' had appeared.

Fishermen (and others) below the Fishermen's Lookout at Beer, *c.* 1910.

Beer, *c.* 1911.

Loading herring at Beer Beech in around 1900. The herring were salted in tubs bearing the fisherman's name, as seen below, and taken by cart to Seaton station.

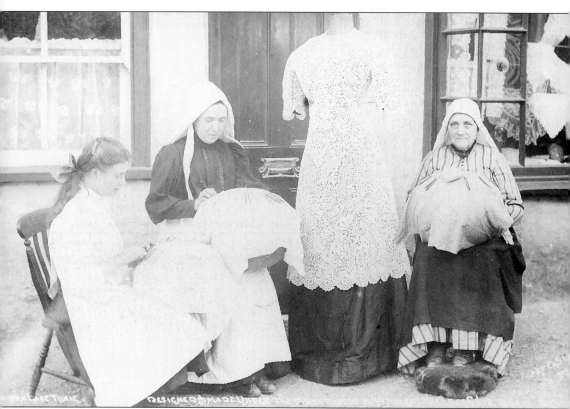

Lace-workers at Beer, *c.* 1899. There is a school of thought that claims Honiton Lace, which was made throughout East Devon, got its name because it was sent to Honiton for despatch by coach to London. On arrival, dealers tended to ask for 'the boxes from Honiton' and that name stuck. Be that as it may, what is known for sure is that a Beer woman, Miss Jane Bidney, had an order placed with her by Queen Victoria for her wedding lace and, according to the *Morning Post*, '200 women worked on it from March to November.' The order gave a fillip to a decaying industry and many members of the Royal Family have either patronised or been given items of Honiton Lace, including Queen Charlotte (George III), Queen Adelaide (William IV), Queen Victoria's daughters, the Princess Royal and Princess Alice, the Princess of Wales (later Edward VII's queen), the Queen Mother, Princess Margaret, Princess Marina, Queen Elizabeth II, and, in a different direction, Mr Speaker Bernard Weatherill.

Oborn's Townsend Garage, Beer, was at the town's (or rather village's) end on the Branscombe road. Mr Dawe, who seems to be about to take delivery of a new van, farmed at Manor Farm on Seaton's Harepath Hill, from where he also ran a milk round.

A Beer lace-maker, seen here in 1880, who was one of the workers on the lace for the neck and sleeve frills, the flounce forming the panelling of the skirt, and the veil for Queen Victoria's wedding dress. It was a common sight, especially on summer days, to see women sitting at the open doors of most cottages in the main street busy making lace.

Fore Street, Beer, *c.* 1903.

The New Inn, Fore Street, Beer, *c.* 1900. The inn, the building on the right behind the two men in the middle of the street, is no longer with us, having become shops. The rather attractive upstairs windows have been replaced.

Dolphin Lane, Beer, *c.* 1904, looking into Clapps Lane.

An aeroplane outside the Old School Room, Beer, in the mid-1930s. It ran out of fuel and made an emergency landing at Southdown Farm. Unable to take off after refuelling, it was removed by one of Clapp's lorries from Seaton (see p. 73). In the picture are Mr Oborn, Tom Clapp and Bill Keate.

The Dolphin Hotel, Beer, displaying its Cyclist Touring Club badge. At the time (*c.* 1907) the proprietor was Mr H. Northcott.

C. Mutter's fish shop in Beer's Fore Street, just above its junction with Deepcut, in the 1920s. There is a fine show of locally caught crabs on offer.

Beer, *c.* 1920.

Beer, *c.* 1910. The shop on the right was Collier's bakery, which was demolished around 1921 when the council houses in The Meadows were completed and the cottagers re-housed there. Today it is an open space used as a car park.

Townsend, Beer, *c.* 1920. At the time, of course, it *was* the 'town's end'.

A naval recovery team, aided by local men, salvage a torpedo at Beer in around 1914.

Seven

Rousdon, Axmouth and the Mouth of the Axe

Rousdon School, 1928.

On Christmas Eve 1839 the Crichard family came home from work to find the path to their cottage beside the cliff at Downlands Farm was sinking. During the night they were forced to evacuate the building when the floors warped and crevices began to appear all over the garden. The path had to be recut before a cart sent by the farmer could reach the cottage and carry their belongings to safety. The following night a coastguard on duty felt the ground thrusting up between his feet and heard a continuous and deafening roar. He moved to safety but was able to watch a great ridge thrusting up out of the sea. In the morning it was discovered that the fields had slid outward for some 300 feet and that an estimated twenty acres and eight million tons had moved. The top drawing, by John Baker of the Alfred House Academy at Ottery St Mary, made soon after the slip, shows people moving on the displaced fields from which the winter wheat was harvested the following autumn. The view of the slip from the sea (below) shows the cottages which slid down and the orchard that went with them. The giant reef forced up out of the sea, and talked about at the time as a possible harbour, was up to a mile long and 400 ft wide in places. Storms soon washed it away, however.

Rousdon, Devon – now erecting for
Sir Henry W. Peek, Bar.ᵗ M.P.
George & Vaughan, Architects.

This drawing by architects George and Vaughan shows the proposed front view of Rousdon Manor, which was completed in 1878 for Sir Henry Peek, whose family fortune was made in groceries and the tea trade towards the end of the previous century. It cost the huge sum of £250,000 but, as his income was said to be in the region of a guinea a minute – £5 million a year – he could more than afford it. There was a six hundred strong workforce on the estate. It was sold in 1938, and Allhallows School, a public school from Honiton, moved in during the spring term.

The meet at Rousdon Manor, *c.* 1904.

Rousdon School, 1921. The pupil at the back on the right is Albert Manley, who would grow up to become as good an authority on the lower Axe as George Pulman himself. Sadly he died in 1996 before his considerable knowledge of East Devon could be recorded. Rousdon School was built by Sir Henry Peek, who introduced what are said to have been the first hot midday meals in England. They cost one penny.

Elizabeth Cross and her daughter Kate in the doorway of their home in Axmouth's Pound Hill in around 1898. The next-door building was Jim Webber's smithy. Today his grandson Roger farms Axe Farm, a dozen yards to the right of this picture.

Pound Hill, Axmouth.

Virtually the same scene thirty years later. A tapped water supply is now available for this end of the village. Note also the general impression of tidiness that has appeared in the road and the houses.

Two views of Chapel Street, Axmouth, in around 1901. This view looks down the road at the post office.

This is the view in the opposite direction. The post office can be clearly seen. It has now returned to this site after many years next to the Ship Inn in the main street. At this time letters for Axmouth went via Colyford rather than the more obvious Seaton (as they do today). There is little truth in the theory that it saved the post office paying the toll for Axmouth Bridge twice per delivery. Earlier Turnpike Trusts, including the Axminster turnpikes of some 100 years before these pictures, allowed mail, the King, MPs and other important people, to pass toll gates without payment.

Axmouth, c. 1909.

Axmouth, c. 1910. The cottages in front of the church have since been demolished. St Michael's church has evidence of Saxon work inside and there is a very handsome Norman south doorway which dates from around 1180. There are other Norman remains inside in the walling of the nave and chancel.

Axmouth, *c*. 1900. The Ship Inn is out of sight on the right. Of special interest is the brook, which has been much altered by flood precaution schemes.

Axmouth, *c*. 1904. The house on the extreme left was the home of Henry Crichard, a wheelwright whose workshop was through the iron gates between the house and the Harbour Inn. The children on the right are almost certainly part of the family of George and Thirza Spiller who lived there. If so, it is Thirza's apron that can just be seen.

Coastguards training below the Axe Bridge between Seaton and Axmouth. It is possible to date this picture to before the First World War because it was then that the coastguards stopped wearing naval uniform.

The River Axe before 1877, when Axmouth Bridge was built. The ferry boat is on the right. At low tide it must have been an unpleasant scramble through the mud for passengers.

Two early nineteenth-century watercolour paintings of the mouth of the River Axe. The top one is the older, if the old harbour walls to the right are any guide. The bottom picture shows three or four buildings nearer the sea which do not appear in the top one. There are masts or sails of ships of some size in both views and these could well be the ships of 100 tons or more that plied twice a week between Seaton and London and unloaded at a pier built by the Hallet family in 1803. The arrival of the railway at Seaton in 1866 finally killed off the harbour's trade and the shingle bar finally won a centuries-old battle with the river, even blocking it for a spell when a particularly fierce south-west gale washed it across the mouth. People, and at least one horse and cart, crossed by means of this temporary ridge. *Pulman's Weekly News* noted that 'The mouth of the Axe, like that of many a human, has been its ruin.'

A 1920 view of the estuary and mouth of the River Axe. Although this card says, 'Seaton, The Harbour', both sides of the river for over a mile upstream from its mouth are in Axmouth parish and an attempt to signpost it as Seaton Harbour in the 1960s met with fierce opposition from Axmouth Parish Council.

The Mouth of Axe by James Townsend. This drawing bears the date 1883, but it is doubtful whether vessels of this size were venturing as far up the river at that time. It is more likely that Townsend, rather than making a completely 'live' drawing, was adding items from the earlier watercolours opposite. The similarity between the two ships is too close to be a coincidence. The buildings at the entrance to the river belonged to the Customs and Excise and were taken down in 1908. Townsend claims that the Axe is 'a small river about 15 miles in length. There is some good fishing to be had – salmon, bass and other.' He may have been right about the fishing – the river is around forty miles long, however!

Seaton. Haven Cliff.

Built in 1877, the Axe Bridge took the the road from Seaton to Axmouth over the Axe. It is seen above not all that long after the arrival of the Seaton & Axmouth (now Axe Cliff) Golf Club in 1894. The golf course was described thus in a 1912 guide book: 'Being only seven minutes walk from the station, the links attract many visitors.' Seven minutes, much of it along Coastguards Lane (surely East Devon's steepest hill open to traffic), is pushing it a bit!

The toll gate at the western end of the bridge in 1904. Although obviously posed, the picture is of great interest as it shows both the open gates and the handsome lights at the Seaton end. The tradesman is paying the gate man for his cart, the two boys, at the (surviving) toll house's door, for their foot passages.

Souvenir

OF

September 30th, 1907,

WHEN

Axmouth Bridge

WAS
DECLARED

FREE OF TOLL FOR EVER

BY

S. Sanders Stephens, Esq.,

J.P., D.L.

ON BEHALF OF THE
DEVON COUNTY COUNCIL.

Axmouth Bridge was opened in 1877 and replaced a ferry that had probably plied for trade since time immemorial. The toll was particularly unpopular with Axmouth people, who had to pay to visit Seaton, and pay again on the way home. Seatonians, with less reason to visit Axmouth, were not so affected. The bridge was the first in England to be built of concrete and has been listed as the youngest 'ancient monument' in the county. It was built with simulated joints to give the impression it was stone-built. Philip Brannon, the designer, originally submitted a design for a single, 100 ft arch, but the Board of Trade (sadly, perhaps) were far from happy about that and the three-arch design was adopted. A new bridge was opened in 1990, but the older bridge, having been designated an ancient monument in 1976, is retained for foot traffic.

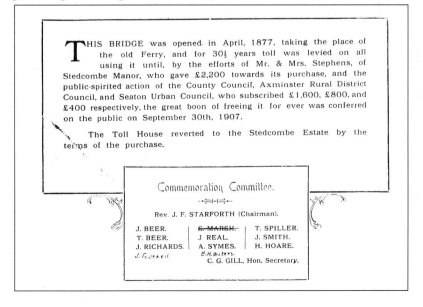

THIS BRIDGE was opened in April, 1877, taking the place of the old Ferry, and for 30½ years toll was levied on all using it until, by the efforts of Mr. & Mrs. Stephens, of Stedcombe Manor, who gave £2,200 towards its purchase, and the public-spirited action of the County Council, Axminster Rural District Council, and Seaton Urban Council, who subscribed £1,600, £800, and £400 respectively, the great boon of freeing it for ever was conferred on the public on September 30th, 1907.

The Toll House reverted to the Stedcombe Estate by the terms of the purchase.

Commemoration Committee.

Rev. J. F. STARFORTH (Chairman).

J. BEER.	E. MARSH.	T. SPILLER.
T. BEER.	J REAL.	J. SMITH.
J. RICHARDS.	A. SYMES.	H. HOARE.
J. Crockett	E.H. Waters.	

C. G. GILL, Hon. Secretary.

Preparing the bonfire on which the Axmouth Bridge toll gates were burnt in 1907.

Seaton from the mouth of the River Axe, c. 1905. Note the almost complete lack of development on Station Road, Trevelyan Road and the East Walk as far as the Beach Hotel (later White Cliff). The buildings just beyond the bridge belong to the railway station and the gasworks.

The new Axe Bridge was opened on 12 October 1990 by Councillor Lt. Col. A.J.M. Drake, Vice Chairman of the Devon County Council's Finance Committee. Axmouth Parish Council were prominent among the dignitaries attending the opening which took place, oddly enough, on the old bridge. They are, back row, left to right: Graham Myers, David Trezise, Douglas Trivett, Michael Clement, Norman Whinfrey. Front: Roger Webber, Cecil Williams, Arthur Ayres (chairman), Mr Baker (clerk), Edwin Newbery, Edward Spiller.

The actual mouth of the river photographed before 1908, when the Customs and Excise buildings were pulled down.

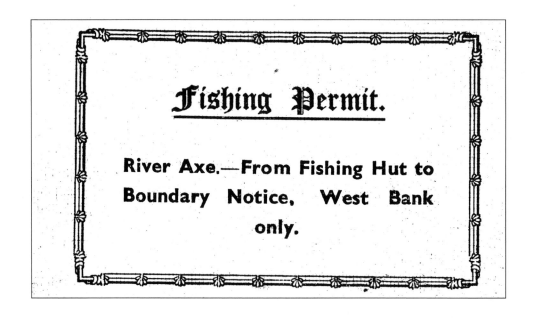

Fishing Permit.

River Axe.—From Fishing Hut to Boundary Notice, West Bank only.

Acknowledgments

We are grateful to Axminster Museum for permission to use some of their old photographs; to the *Express and Echo*, who allowed us to browse through their archives and make use of items from their fine collection of photographs; and to Len Northcott of Seaton, for permission to use many items from his magnificent collection of pictures of old Seaton, Rousdon, Axmouth and Beer. Len is one of those (regrettably few) people who not only collect old photographs, but also goes out and photographs the same scenes as they are today.

We have been privileged, through his son Gilbert, to have access to the family's collection of the pictures of the late Charles Humphries, the celebrated Axminster photographer whose work on the town and its immediate surroundings is probably better known today for the many excellent postcards he produced.

Frank Soanes gave pictures and also his time to talk about a Colyton he so obviously loves, while Elsie Pady and her son Graham, who also lent pictures, told us much about a river that Elsie's late husband Roy spent so much time exploring and photographing, including an aerial video of the river from its source to the sea. Elsie Selway of Colyton was a mine of information on her beloved home town.

Others to lend us their old pictures, and to whom we would like to say thankyou are: Jack Banfield, Joyce Berry, Mike Clement, Jim Cross, Rosemary Frazier, John Godfrey of the Seaton Book Centre, Frank Huddy, Ted Humphrey, Derek and Denise Loud, George Mabon and Seaton Red Cross, the late Albert Manley, whose reminiscences of the Axe valley could have, and should have, filled a book, Arch Mitchell, Eileen 'Lan' Mutter, Tom and Bill Richards, Bill Snell, George Tatham, Sheilagh and Peggy Taylor, and Bert Trivett.

Some research has been necessary at both Seaton and Axminster libraries, and the staff at both, as always, have been even more courteous and helpful than duty demands.

In a different direction we are grateful to Jack Thomas, the Uplyme historian, for his excellent introduction, and to the staff at Chalford Publishing Company, especially Simon Thraves, for putting up with us.